VANITY

A very peculiar history

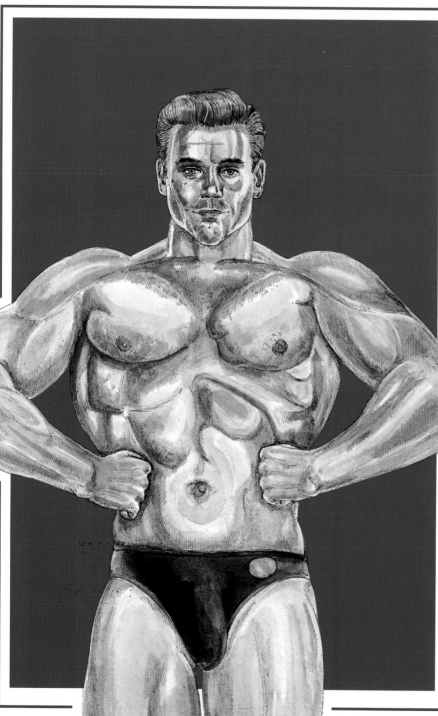

SERIES EDITOR	DAVID SALARIYA
BOOK EDITOR	PENNY CLARKE
ASSISTANT	APRIL McCROSKIE
ARTISTS	DAVID ANTRAM
	RAY BURROWS
	VIRGINIA GRAY
	NICK HEWETSON
	BARBARA LOFTUS
	GORDON MUNRO
	LEE PETERS
	CAROLYN SCRACE

DAVID SALARIYA has created many new series of books for publishers worldwide. In 1989 he established the Salariya Book Company. He lives in England with his wife, the illustrator Shirley Willis.

VICKI POWER is an American writer, editor, and journalist who has lived in Britain since 1985. She is an honors graduate of Amherst College in Amherst, Massachusetts.

First published in 1995 by Franklin Watts

Franklin Watts
95 Madison Avenue, New York, NY 10016

Library of Congress Cataloging-in-Publication Data

Power, Vicki.
    Vanity / written by Vicki Power : created and designed by David Salariya.
        p. cm. – (A very peculiar history)
        Includes index.
        Summary: Presents an overview of trends, customs, and fashions relating to the pursuit of physical beauty from ancient times to the present including such topics as body shape, clothing, cosmetics, and hair fashions.
    ISBN 0-531-14356-2 (lib. bdg.)–
    ISBN 0-531-15273-1 (pbk.)
    1. Body, Human–Social aspects–Juvenile literature. 2. Body image–Juvenile literature. 3. Costume–Juvenile literature. 4. Cosmetics–Juvenile literature. 5 Body marking–Juvenile literature. 6. Pride and vanity–Juvenile literature. [1. Body image. 2. Beauty, Personal.] I. Title. II. Series
GT495.P69 1995
391'.6–dc20   94-40133
                                              CIP
                                              AC

Printed in Belgium

VANITY

A very peculiar history

Written by
VICKI POWER

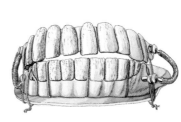

Created and designed by
DAVID SALARIYA

FRANKLIN WATTS

NEW YORK • CHICAGO • LONDON • TORONTO • SYDNEY

CONTENTS

INTRODUCTION

VANITY IS LARGELY viewed as a negative term. It conjures up images of notorious self-admirers like Cinderella's ugly stepsisters and Narcissus, the boy in love with his own reflection. But these characters carried vanity to the extreme. Most people would probably admit to a certain amount of self-regard, in looks or clothes, accomplishments or possessions.

The pursuit of beauty is not new. Humans have always sought to change themselves for the better, as part of an ongoing quest to become more beautiful, attract the opposite sex, follow fashion, and show group membership. Why else were ancient Minoans strapping themselves into tight girdles and ancient Romans plucking out all their body hair, except to improve their looks and be admired?

Many of the beauty aids and rituals used over the centuries now seem ridiculous. It's hard to imagine that a false nose or mouse-skin eyebrows could really have enhanced anyone's appearance, but concepts of beauty change. Fat women today are likely to incur ridicule, but their 17th-century counterparts were considered so beautiful that they were regularly painted by the great artists of the time. Women today may scoff at the idea of wearing a corset to achieve a better figure but would not shrink from the surgeon's knife or a fad diet to achieve the same effect.

This book is dedicated to revealing the unusual and sometimes bizarre efforts employed over the centuries in the pursuit of beauty, not forgetting that many men and women paid a high price to achieve it.

THE IDEAL BODY

A beautiful body is as much of a fashion statement as the latest clothes.

The Willendorf Venus and other ancient maternal statues celebrated ample women.

THROUGHOUT THE AGES, men and especially women have altered their natural body shape in order to achieve the look currently in vogue. Nearly every culture has had its own concept of the ideal body—the ancient Greeks prized a lean, muscular physique (even in women), while Edwardian Britain liked S-shaped women. Today's superthin catwalk models would not have been admired during the 17th century, for example, when rounded and fleshy women were chosen as subjects for paintings by Rubens and Rembrandt.

Sometimes attention has focused on the overall body shape, sometimes on one particular attribute.

In the 18th century, European men drew attention to their shapely calves, while a century later, German men proudly displayed their large stomachs.

Body ideals can change even from generation to generation. The bosom, waist, buttocks, and legs have all been in or out of fashion. Women (mostly) have subjected themselves to endless bodily transformations: ridiculous contraptions have been invented and dangerous fads followed to force their bodies into fashionable shapes.

Before cellulite was a dirty word, Rubens painted fleshy women in "The Three Graces."

A small bust, big tummy, and an S-shaped body were admired in 15th-century Europe. The figure was achieved by chest-flattening corsets that pushed the abdomen out.

A large backside has occasionally been admired in Western cultures. It was suggested by the bustle of the 1870s and by modern high-heeled shoes that simulate it by throwing the spine out of alignment.

Fatness, long admired in tribal cultures, was a status symbol among European and American men in the late 19th century.

(left) The wasp-waisted, S-shaped figure of 1900 was achieved by wearing a rigid corset that distorted the spine's alignment.

(right) By the 1920s large busts were out – women wore chest-flattening corsets to achieve a concave, boyish look.

WESTERNERS STILL prize the athletic body ideal inherited from the ancient Greeks. Modern body-builders strive for an exaggerated version of that look through strenuous exercise and even by taking drugs, such as anabolic steroids.

The statue of Diskobolos of c.450 B.C. (right) captures the ancient Greek ideal of the lean, muscular body.

In 1966, Twiggy launched a body image that has endured. The appeal of her adolescent body fueled the slimming industry and put millions of young women on a diet.

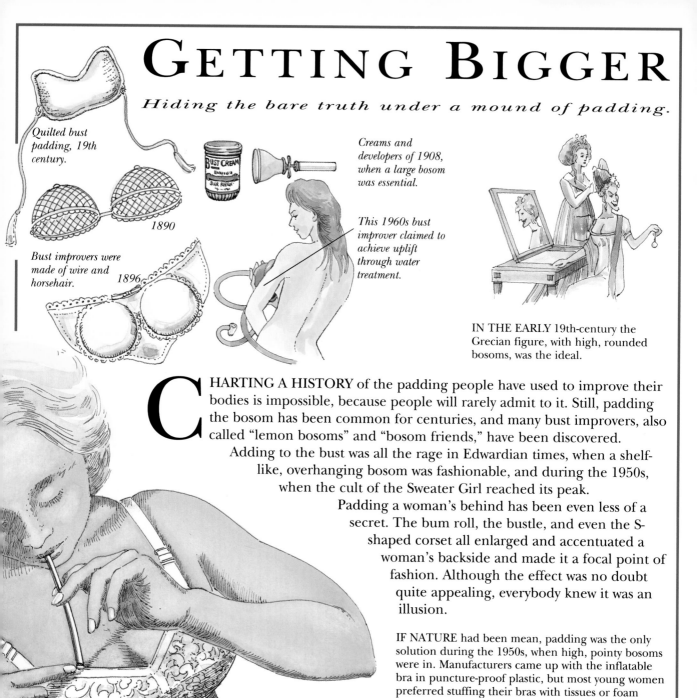

GETTING BIGGER

Hiding the bare truth under a mound of padding.

Quilted bust padding, 19th century.

1890

Bust improvers were made of wire and horsehair.

1896

Creams and developers of 1908, when a large bosom was essential.

BUST CREAM

This 1960s bust improver claimed to achieve uplift through water treatment.

IN THE EARLY 19th-century the Grecian figure, with high, rounded bosoms, was the ideal.

CHARTING A HISTORY of the padding people have used to improve their bodies is impossible, because people will rarely admit to it. Still, padding the bosom has been common for centuries, and many bust improvers, also called "lemon bosoms" and "bosom friends," have been discovered.

Adding to the bust was all the rage in Edwardian times, when a shelf-like, overhanging bosom was fashionable, and during the 1950s, when the cult of the Sweater Girl reached its peak.

Padding a woman's behind has been even less of a secret. The bum roll, the bustle, and even the S-shaped corset all enlarged and accentuated a woman's backside and made it a focal point of fashion. Although the effect was no doubt quite appealing, everybody knew it was an illusion.

IF NATURE had been mean, padding was the only solution during the 1950s, when high, pointy bosoms were in. Manufacturers came up with the inflatable bra in puncture-proof plastic, but most young women preferred stuffing their bras with tissues or foam rubber pads called "falsies."

Before and after

pad gives "uplift"

THE BUSTLE was fashionable from 1870 to 1900. When worn with a corset, it produced the illusion of a small-waisted, large-bottomed woman, a combination not found in nature.

bustle with springs

whalebone bustle

girdle

FASHIONS AFTER World War II accentuated the bosom. The 1950s gave rise to the "Sweater Girl" (above and left), so-called because she wore a pointy, push-up bra under a tight sweater. Film stars such as Jane Russell made the look popular.

"The Bum Shop," a cartoon of 1785, made fun of women who padded their buttocks in order to look fashionable.

Foam rubber pads exaggerate the buttocks and "give you that rounded look," claimed an advertisement in 1959.

foam rubber pads

MEN HAVE LARGELY escaped fashionable additions, though 18th- and 19th-century dandies wore corsets to achieve the correct hourglass look. The peasecod belly of the 16th century simulated a protruding stomach, but surely the most ostentatious piece of male padding has been the codpiece.

(left) The fashionable Italian gentleman of 1565 wore a prominent codpiece.

Shoulder pads for women first appeared in the 1940s. In the 1980s they symbolized the businesswoman.

codpiece

GETTING SMALLER

Devices designed to rein in women and briefly, men.

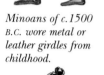

Minoans of c.1500 B.C. wore metal or leather girdles from childhood.

To achieve the boyish figure admired in ancient Greece, women bound their breasts.

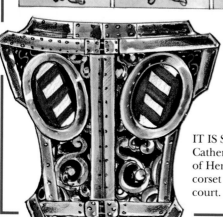

In the 15th century, corsets were worn high to flatten the bust. When lying down women even put lead plates onto their chests.

FOR CENTURIES swelling chests have been flattened, prominent tummies pulled in, and waists severely squeezed by stays and corsets designed to make women smaller and help them fit into the fashionable clothes of the day. Corsets became widely used in Europe from the 15th century, but they were worn as long ago as 2000 B.C. The ancient Minoans wore tight girdles around the waist, a practice still followed today by some Papuans of New Guinea. Women of ancient Greece and Rome flattened the bust by wrapping bandages around it. Corsets reappeared in Europe during the 15th century, and from the 18th century they were more rigid and tightly laced than ever. A movement for healthier clothes and women's emancipation led to the discarding of rigid underclothes in the early 20th century. But even when the harmful effects of corsets became well-known in the 19th century, their continued use was justified on the moral grounds that corsets controlled women's seductive powers. In reality, many corsets emphasized the bust and bottom.

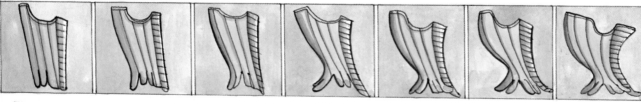

In these drawings from his "Analysis of Beauty" (1753), English artist William Hogarth admired corsets for their own beauty.

18th-century Circassian girls from northeast of the Black Sea had to wear leather corsets from age seven until their wedding.

IT IS SAID that the fashionable Catherine de Médici (1519–1589), wife of Henry II of France, invented the iron corset (left) to slim the women in her court.

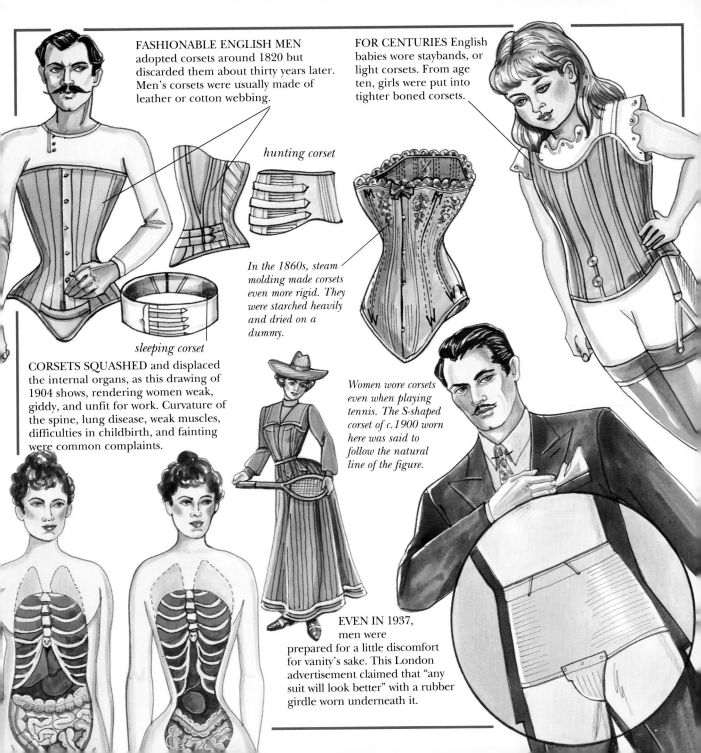

FASHIONABLE ENGLISH MEN adopted corsets around 1820 but discarded them about thirty years later. Men's corsets were usually made of leather or cotton webbing.

FOR CENTURIES English babies wore staybands, or light corsets. From age ten, girls were put into tighter boned corsets.

hunting corset

sleeping corset

In the 1860s, steam molding made corsets even more rigid. They were starched heavily and dried on a dummy.

CORSETS SQUASHED and displaced the internal organs, as this drawing of 1904 shows, rendering women weak, giddy, and unfit for work. Curvature of the spine, lung disease, weak muscles, difficulties in childbirth, and fainting were common complaints.

Women wore corsets even when playing tennis. The S-shaped corset of c.1900 worn here was said to follow the natural line of the figure.

EVEN IN 1937, men were prepared for a little discomfort for vanity's sake. This London advertisement claimed that "any suit will look better" with a rubber girdle worn underneath it.

CHANGING SHAPE

Putting on the pressure to build a better body.

Babies of Chinook natives of North America had their brows flattened in these appliances.

Padaung women of Burma stretch their necks with brass rings as a status symbol and sign of submission to their husbands. If the rings were taken off, their necks would be unable to support the weight of their heads.

The heads of Mangbetu baby girls are wrapped in leaves to form an elongated skull, considered to be beautiful.

LIP PLUGS add beauty to the mouth and usually carry symbolic significance. To the Suya people of Brazil (right), lip plugs emphasize the importance of speaking. In other cultures, ear disks and eye decoration symbolize listening and seeing.

Humans have always deformed their bodies to make them conform to an ideal. Tribal societies have a very long tradition of molding their bodies into unusual shapes that are considered beautiful and may also symbolize a commitment to religious or moral beliefs. Societies that routinely practice body shaping consider the body in its natural state to be unattractive.

Head shaping and leg binding may seem barbaric and grotesque to many Westerners, yet the Western custom of wearing corsets from a young age to produce a tiny waist (discussed on pages 12-13) was as primitive and painful a body alteration as any practiced by tribal people. Molding the skull of children from birth to form a more pleasing shape has been practiced for centuries in cultures as diverse as ancient Egypt, 19th-century France, and Africa.

Plastic surgery and drastic dieting have now replaced corset wearing as the West's way of producing an acceptable body.

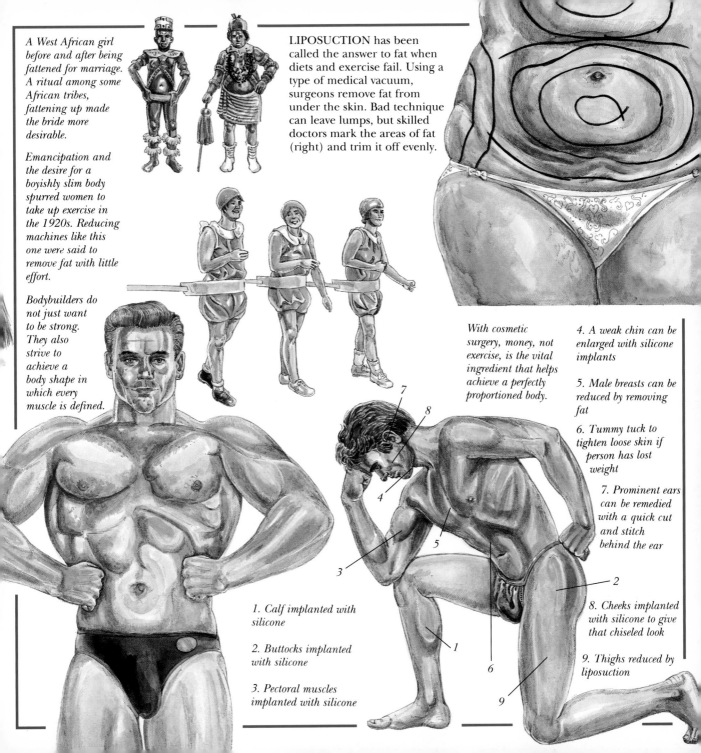

A West African girl before and after being fattened for marriage. A ritual among some African tribes, fattening up made the bride more desirable.

Emancipation and the desire for a boyishly slim body spurred women to take up exercise in the 1920s. Reducing machines like this one were said to remove fat with little effort.

Bodybuilders do not just want to be strong. They also strive to achieve a body shape in which every muscle is defined.

LIPOSUCTION has been called the answer to fat when diets and exercise fail. Using a type of medical vacuum, surgeons remove fat from under the skin. Bad technique can leave lumps, but skilled doctors mark the areas of fat (right) and trim it off evenly.

With cosmetic surgery, money, not exercise, is the vital ingredient that helps achieve a perfectly proportioned body.

1. Calf implanted with silicone

2. Buttocks implanted with silicone

3. Pectoral muscles implanted with silicone

4. A weak chin can be enlarged with silicone implants

5. Male breasts can be reduced by removing fat

6. Tummy tuck to tighten loose skin if person has lost weight

7. Prominent ears can be remedied with a quick cut and stitch behind the ear

8. Cheeks implanted with silicone to give that chiseled look

9. Thighs reduced by liposuction

CHANGING COLOR

A fine color enhances social standing.

In Babylon c.3000 B.C., people painted their faces with white lead, a custom followed in Europe until the 18th century.

Roman women whitened their faces and arms with lead or chalk.

Arsenic was used to whiten skin. In 18th-century Italy a scandal erupted when 600 men died after getting too close to their wives, whose faces were coated with arsenic.

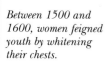

Between 1500 and 1600, women feigned youth by whitening their chests.

Queen Elizabeth I's skin was ruined by a lead-based white face paste.

LILY-WHITE SKIN has been prized by men and women throughout history. It hinted at high social standing and money enough to avoid having to venture outside to work. The weather-beaten skin of peasants and other outdoor laborers was considered coarse and unattractive.

To achieve the pale look, not only on their faces but also on their necks and bosoms, women painted themselves with poisonous lead, scrubbed and bleached their skin, chalked and powdered their faces, and swallowed dangerous mixtures. In the 18th century, Frenchwomen even applied leeches in the hope of draining away their color.

All that changed in the 1920s and 1930s. Emancipation allowed women to shed corsets and wear more daring swimsuits. By this time most people worked indoors, in factories and offices, so white skin no longer had social status. A tan became the ultimate fashion accessory, a sign of money and the leisure to spend time on the beach. Recent reports of skin cancer and premature aging due to overexposure have helped to discourage sunbathing.

17th-CENTURY upper-class European women and men protected their white skin by wearing masks outdoors. Some masks were kept in place by a button held in the mouth.

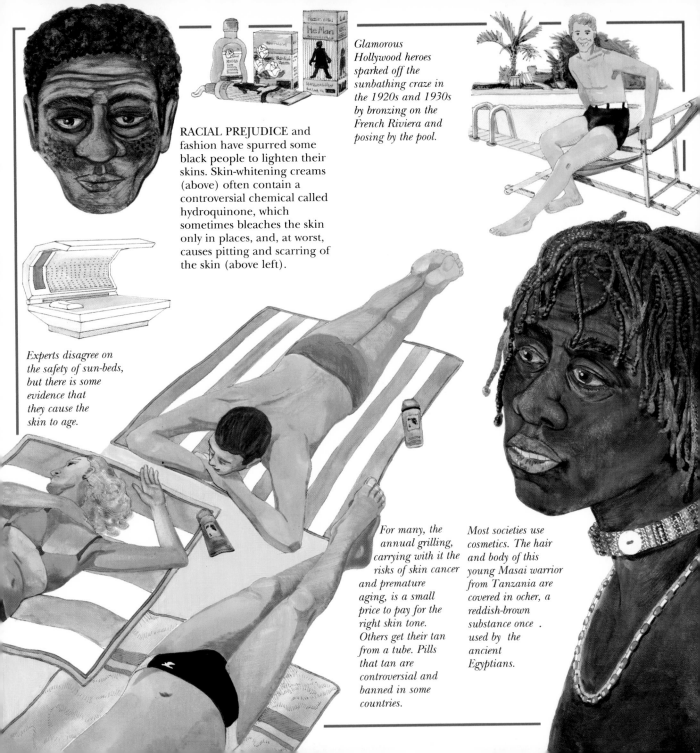

RACIAL PREJUDICE and fashion have spurred some black people to lighten their skins. Skin-whitening creams (above) often contain a controversial chemical called hydroquinone, which sometimes bleaches the skin only in places, and, at worst, causes pitting and scarring of the skin (above left).

Glamorous Hollywood heroes sparked off the sunbathing craze in the 1920s and 1930s by bronzing on the French Riviera and posing by the pool.

Experts disagree on the safety of sun-beds, but there is some evidence that they cause the skin to age.

For many, the annual grilling, carrying with it the risks of skin cancer and premature aging, is a small price to pay for the right skin tone. Others get their tan from a tube. Pills that tan are controversial and banned in some countries.

Most societies use cosmetics. The hair and body of this young Masai warrior from Tanzania are covered in ocher, a reddish-brown substance once . used by the ancient Egyptians.

THE ART OF THE NEEDLE

Natives and nonconformists share a passion for tattooing.

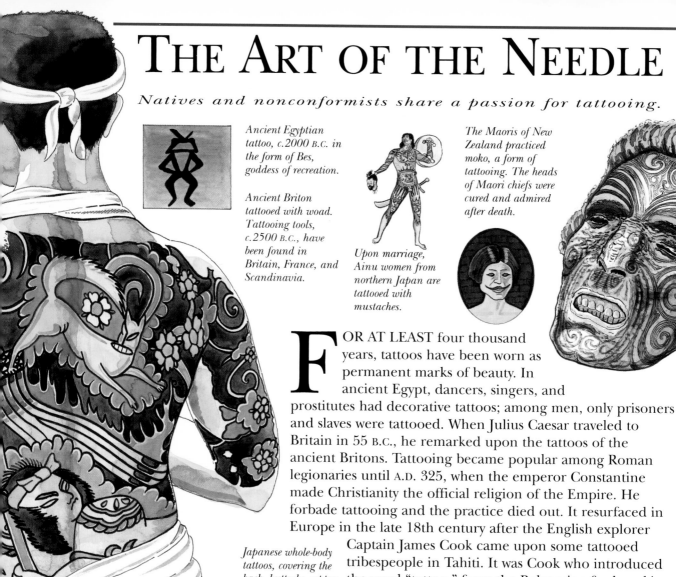

Ancient Egyptian tattoo, c.2000 B.C. in the form of Bes, goddess of recreation.

Ancient Briton tattooed with woad. Tattooing tools, c.2500 B.C., have been found in Britain, France, and Scandinavia.

The Maoris of New Zealand practiced moko, a form of tattooing. The heads of Maori chiefs were cured and admired after death.

Upon marriage, Ainu women from northern Japan are tattooed with mustaches.

Japanese whole-body tattoos, covering the back, buttocks, upper thighs, and upper arms, clothe the naked body, which in Japan is not thought to be beautiful. An art gallery dedicated to irezumi contains complete skins of tattooed men.

F OR AT LEAST four thousand years, tattoos have been worn as permanent marks of beauty. In ancient Egypt, dancers, singers, and prostitutes had decorative tattoos; among men, only prisoners and slaves were tattooed. When Julius Caesar traveled to Britain in 55 B.C., he remarked upon the tattoos of the ancient Britons. Tattooing became popular among Roman legionaries until A.D. 325, when the emperor Constantine made Christianity the official religion of the Empire. He forbade tattooing and the practice died out. It resurfaced in Europe in the late 18th century after the English explorer Captain James Cook came upon some tattooed tribespeople in Tahiti. It was Cook who introduced the word "tattoo," from the Polynesian for knocking or striking, *tatau.*

Yet tattooing has flourished for centuries in Japan and the South Sea islands. Japanese tattooing, called *irezumi,* was at its peak in the 17th and 18th centuries, but some men still have whole-body tattoos. Among South Sea islands people, tattoos beautify and show community membership.

Client and tattoo master decide on a design, from historical Japanese books.

The tattoo master carefully draws the design on the client's body with a felt-tip pen.

The client inspects the design and can make changes, but the master always has the final say.

THE TATTOO'S OUTLINE is incised using traditional needles and *sumi*, a black ink. Then the colors are applied. Varying the number of needles and depth they are inserted alters light and shade.

Like all tattooing, irezumi is painful, and it can take a year or more to complete a design.

When a British army officer was unable to find work after World War I, he was tattooed with a green, zebra-like design and worked for circuses as "The Great Omi."

(below) Two examples of Burchett's work.

George Burchett (1872–1953) studied tattooing in Japan. He had aristocrats and disfigured soldiers as clients.

coronation tattoo

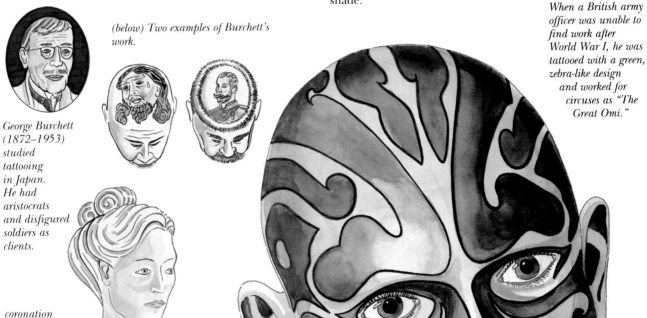

In 1901, coronation tattoos were the rage among rich London women. Others had a tattoo artist redden their lips and darken their eyebrows.

CUTS AND SLICES

The body as a canvas to be decorated.

The Tiv of Nigeria rub charcoal into scars to make them stand out.

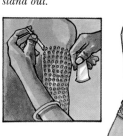

Yanomami men of northeastern South America enjoy fights in which they throw 7-foot (2-m) long wooden cabers at each other's heads. The men display their scars by shaving off the hair around them.

The Nubans of Sudan scarify by lifting the skin with a hook, then slicing it with a blade. A woman's back is scarified when her first child is weaned.

SCARIFICATION, or cutting the skin to create raised scars, is a form of body decoration practiced mostly by dark-skinned people of Africa. (Tattooing does not show up on dark skin.) Intricate geometric patterns of scars enhance beauty and show group membership. Being scarred is sometimes a rite of passage; a young person proves courage by enduring pain in order to achieve the scars. The most pronounced scars, which cause the most pain, are usually considered the most attractive. Scarification also shows that a person has entered a new phase in life—among the Bangwa of the Cameroon, women were scarified on the chest and stomach before marriage, and on the back after the birth of their first child. Many scarification rituals have died out since missionaries disapproved of and governments banned them.

Scars received in battle have been considered a mark of valor, and wounds received in duels are proudly displayed as proof of manliness.

Piercing the nose or ears is common in many cultures and is usually done to display jewelry or ornaments.

The scars left by hanging buffalo skulls from the skin were marks of initiation among the Cheyenne Indians.

19TH-CENTURY German students held duels just to get face scars. Red wine poured into the wound exaggerated the scarring.

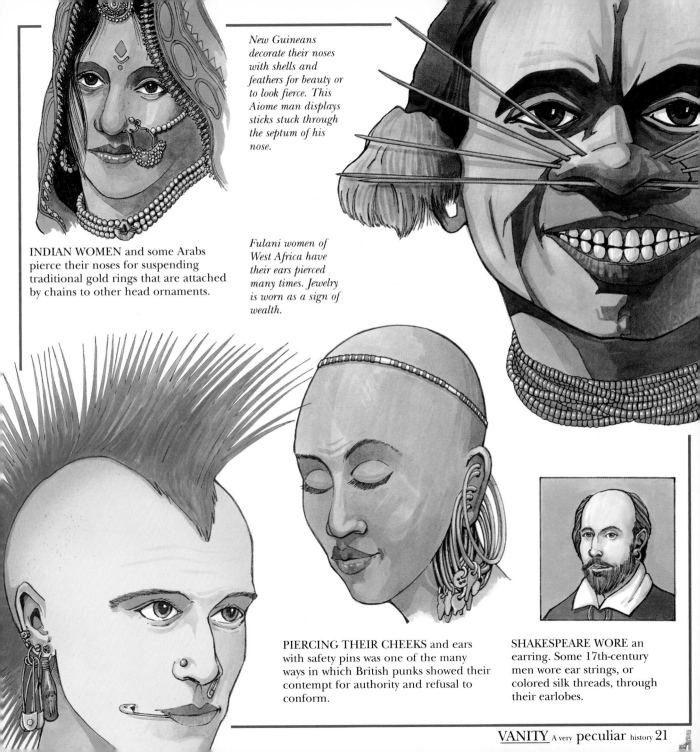

New Guineans decorate their noses with shells and feathers for beauty or to look fierce. This Aiome man displays sticks stuck through the septum of his nose.

INDIAN WOMEN and some Arabs pierce their noses for suspending traditional gold rings that are attached by chains to other head ornaments.

Fulani women of West Africa have their ears pierced many times. Jewelry is worn as a sign of wealth.

PIERCING THEIR CHEEKS and ears with safety pins was one of the many ways in which British punks showed their contempt for authority and refusal to conform.

SHAKESPEARE WORE an earring. Some 17th-century men wore ear strings, or colored silk threads, through their earlobes.

POWDER AND PAINT

When barefaced cheeks are not good enough.

The ancient Egyptians used kohl, a black paste, around their eyes.

By the 4th century B.C., Greek women wore makeup.

A peddler of 1491 sells makeup to lower-class women.

RARELY SATISFIED with their natural appearance, women and men have been slapping on paint and powder for centuries. The ancient Egyptians were among the first people to use makeup for purely cosmetic purposes. They decorated the eye, considered to be the mirror of the soul. In other cultures, makeup has been used to emphasize different facial features—Renaissance women prized porcelain-white complexions, while 1940s movie stars created sensual mouths with bright, shiny lipstick.

Fashions in makeup have inevitably followed social trends. Ostentatious Roman makeup gave way to near abstinence from makeup during the sober Middle Ages. The excesses of the court of King Louis XIV of France (ruled 1643–1715) were epitomized by the elaborate makeup, clothes, and coiffures of the period. All this gave way to a much simpler style after the French Revolution (1789–1799).

Over the centuries, makeup has caused churchmen to rail against vanity, and husbands to accuse made-up wives of deceiving them about their looks. Books have been published on the vulgarity of cosmetics. In 1770 the British Parliament even passed a law stating that any woman who betrayed a man into marriage by the use of makeup would be subject to the same penalties as for witchcraft, and that the marriage would be null and void. Yet most women preferred to incur the wrath of the moralists rather than show the world an unfashionable face and continued to devote considerable attention to their toilette.

Two ancient Egyptian recipes for dyeing the eyebrows: (1) crocodile dung mixed with honey that has been dissolved in onion water; (2) ass's liver warmed in oil with opium.

Japanese women in the 18th century reddened their lips and powdered their skin.

THIS PORTRAIT of Queen Elizabeth I, in middle age, shows that she tried to simulate the translucent skin of a younger woman by painting blue veins on her forehead over ceruse (white lead makeup). The ceruse ate into her flesh, so she had to apply it more and more thickly.

Metallic makeup could turn a romantic tryst into a humiliation. Here, sulfur from the coal fire reacts with vapors in the air to turn pink rouge black. Another 18th-century rouge turned yellow if a person chewed a clove and breathed on the woman's face.

Until the 20th century, rouge was often made with dangerous metals. The Romans used fucus, a paint made from mercury. Red lead was popular until the 19th century, as was a mixture of brimstone and mercury.

DURING WORLD WAR II, stockings were at a premium, so British women smeared makeup on their legs to imitate them. A friend then drew a straight black line down the back of each leg to simulate stocking seams.

In the 1890s Sarah Bernhardt revived the lavish use of makeup.

Women copied Garbo's sultry-eyed, pale-faced look in the 1930s.

Audrey Hepburn set a 1950s trend for heavily lined eyes and brows.

Ancient Egyptian cosmetic spoon made of alabaster and slate.

Egyptian wooden cosmetics box from a grave, c.1400 B.C.

The fashionable Macaroni of 1772 wore thick white makeup, rouge, and lipstick. Macaronis were young Englishmen in the 1770s who dressed in exaggerated styles.

A recipe for making "Puppidog Water" for the complexion, 1700, began: "Take a fat Puppidog of 9 days old, and kill it. ... Take the blood ... and break the legs and head, with all the liver and Innards. ..."

A 1940s gold-tone, hand-shaped powder compact.

TEETHING PAINS

Stopping the rot in the days before toothpaste.

FALSE TEETH were worn as early as 700 B.C., but for vanity's sake only, as they were not functional. The Etruscans made gold bridges (left) to hold false teeth, while the Phoenicians wired false teeth to natural teeth (left, above).

Parisian surgeon Pierre Fauchard (1678–1761) invented dentures held together with springs, which stayed in place by pressing against the gums. Force was needed just to close the mouth. George Washington (below right) wore them.

ROTTEN TEETH and a gummy smile have blighted the face of many would-be beauties, a problem that may have spurred even the earliest cultures to make dentures. The Phoenicians and Etruscans tied or wired teeth onto patients' natural teeth. Romans wore wooden false teeth "as black as pitch," according to one report. From the 16th century, Europeans experimented with false teeth made from ivory, silver, mother-of-pearl, and porcelain, and they plundered battlefields and slaughterhouses for teeth from human and animal corpses. Though most early dentures fooled no one, were often murderously uncomfortable and were usually removed for eating, the fashionable European élite staunchly bore the pain for the sake of vanity. In the 18th century a barbaric craze swept Europe and America for transplanting the teeth of healthy young peasants into the mouths of rich, toothless aristocrats. The fad died out as false teeth improved.

Ornate cases containing a gold toothpick were worn as jewelry during the Renaissance, when it was acceptable to pick one's teeth at the dinner table.

The neat set of pearly whites sought after by Europeans, however, has not always been prized elsewhere. Fashionable Chinese and Japanese women and some Native Americans blackened their teeth, Hindus colored them red, and Middle Eastern women stained their teeth yellow, purple, and blue.

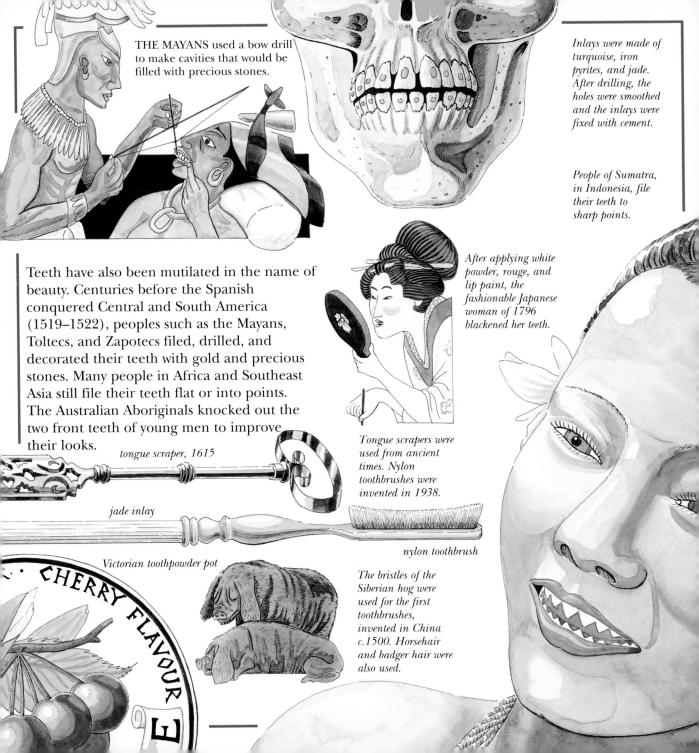

THE MAYANS used a bow drill to make cavities that would be filled with precious stones.

Inlays were made of turquoise, iron pyrites, and jade. After drilling, the holes were smoothed and the inlays were fixed with cement.

People of Sumatra, in Indonesia, file their teeth to sharp points.

Teeth have also been mutilated in the name of beauty. Centuries before the Spanish conquered Central and South America (1519–1522), peoples such as the Mayans, Toltecs, and Zapotecs filed, drilled, and decorated their teeth with gold and precious stones. Many people in Africa and Southeast Asia still file their teeth flat or into points. The Australian Aboriginals knocked out the two front teeth of young men to improve their looks.

After applying white powder, rouge, and lip paint, the fashionable Japanese woman of 1796 blackened her teeth.

tongue scraper, 1615

jade inlay

Tongue scrapers were used from ancient times. Nylon toothbrushes were invented in 1938.

nylon toothbrush

Victorian toothpowder pot

CHERRY FLAVOUR

The bristles of the Siberian hog were used for the first toothbrushes, invented in China c.1500. Horsehair and badger hair were also used.

A PRESENTABLE FACE

Facing up to the whims of fashion.

MAKEUP HAS undoubtedly been the favored form of facial beautification throughout the ages, but certain imperfections could not be disguised by even the heaviest application of white lead. The ancient Romans glued small patches of material on their faces to cover up flaws, a practice that reemerged with a vengeance in the 17th century when fashionable Europeans disguised the ravages of smallpox with up to 20 velvet or taffeta patches worn at once. False eyebrows and lashes were worn in Europe from the 18th century, and, almost unbelievably, false noses of gold and porcelain. Even the eyeballs have been subjected to beauty rituals. The ancient Egyptians, Romans, and Persians applied antimony sulfide to their eyes to make them glitter. Today, in the Far East, a popular operation will make eyes rounder and more European-looking.

In the 19th century, scores of enterprising inventors marketed facial appliances which, they claimed, would melt away double chins and rein in protuberant noses. Today, cosmetic surgery can rebuild the nose, puff up the lips, tuck in the chin, and remove years of wear and tear.

This peddler of 1640 sold patches of velvet that hid spots and craters. Women applied them with care, as their position indicated to men their availability and mood (below).

Here be your new Fashions Mistris

BEDOUINS stained their eye whites blue with kohl, while 16th-century European women put belladonna into their eyes to dilate the pupils.

A fad among 18th-century English women was to shave off their eyebrows and apply false ones made of mouse skin. They often came loose during lively conversation.

Belladonna

Bedouin

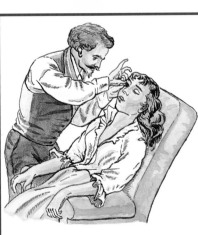

IN 1882 in the United States, skimpy eyelashes could be thickened by having false ones sewn onto the eyelids.

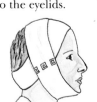

This face-lift comes from a book written in 1925 by the father of modern cosmetic surgery, C. C. Miller.

As the search for youth and physical perfection grows ever more urgent, face-lifts have become more common. (right) A standard face-lift in which excess facial skin is trimmed and fat bags are removed from the eyelids.

This U.S. "face–lifter" of the 1960s claimed to produce a firm chin line if the user bit down on it for 60 seconds a day.

(left) Appliances like the "Youth Molde" band of 1935 claimed to cure double chins if worn regularly.

FALSE EYELASHES returned to the fashion scene in the 1960s, but now they could be glued on at home.

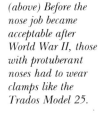

(above) Before the nose job became acceptable after World War II, those with protuberant noses had to wear clamps like the Trados Model 25.

The Claxton Ear-Cap, advertised in England in 1903, claimed to cure sticking out ears when worn in bed.

Before surgery the skin is cleaned and marked to show where to cut.

The skin is loosened, then excess skin trimmed away and stitched.

Eyelids are cut and the bags of fat removed from the upper lid.

Eyelid skin must be stitched carefully to make sure the line doesn't show.

Special strips hold down the pullout stitches near the eye. Operation over.

TOO MUCH HAIR

When hirsute does not suit, pain is taken to pluck and tweeze.

IT IS NOT ONLY IN THE 20TH CENTURY that the removal of excess body hair has become fashionable. The discovery of Bronze Age tweezers reveals that people were plucking stray hairs five thousand years ago. A hairless body was mandatory for high-ranking officials in ancient Egypt, and in ancient Greece body hair was a fashion blight. In 17th-century Europe, women made hair-removing solutions from burned leeches and frogs' blood. Women also altered the shape of their eyebrows and plucked their hairlines, which rose and fell with changing fashions.

Facial hair for men has gone in and out of fashion. The earliest cave drawings depict both bearded and unbearded men, evidence that even early man shaved. Egyptian and Assyrian men shaved their heads and faces, and a Roman, Scipio Africanus (c.235–183 B.C.), has gone down in history as the first man to shave daily.

Barbershops were social gathering places from the time of the Greeks, c.500 B.C., and remained so in Europe until the 20th century, when the safety razor replaced the straight, "cutthroat" razor used since biblical times. By incorporating metal guards to stop the user cutting his throat, the safety razor meant that a steady hand was no longer necessary for safe shaving.

Eyebrow styles: ancient Sumeria (above), and 11th-century Japan (below).

Marlene Dietrich (above) plucked her brows; other women shaved theirs.

Tweezers through the ages: a) Denmark, c.2000 B.C; b) ancient Egypt, c.2000 B.C.; c) Roman A.D.100; d) Frankish, 5th-8th century; e) modern.

Roman emperor Julius Caesar (100– 44 B.C.) was obsessive about plucking out his body hair.

Greek men believed that a hairless body was more hygienic and attractive.

15th-century European women plucked or shaved their hairlines to form a fashionable high forehead.

(right) Japanese women shaving, 19th century. Bearded women have long been freak attractions.

Today Western fashion dictates that women have almost no body hair. Waxing (left), sugaring, shaving, and electrolysis remove excess body hair.

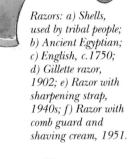

Razors: a) Shells, used by tribal people; b) Ancient Egyptian; c) English, c.1750; d) Gillette razor, 1902; e) Razor with sharpening strap, 1940s; f) Razor with comb guard and shaving cream, 1951.

A U.S. barbershop, 1861. Barbers have existed since biblical times. In ancient Egypt they were itinerant, shaving customers in the street. For many centuries, barbers also performed dentistry and minor surgery.

TOO LITTLE HAIR

Remedies to stop the mane attraction from receding.

JUDGING BY THE HUGE ARRAY of recipes for hair restorers that have been handed down over the centuries, baldness was a social embarrassment even six thousand years ago. In 4000 B.C., one balding woman concocted her own home remedy from a combination of dogs' paws, asses' hooves, and dates, ground together, cooked in oil, then rubbed on the scalp. How well it worked is not known, but through history the scalp has been bathed in all manner of substances to encourage hair growth. Wigs and even paint have been used to help men and women to disguise thinning locks.

In today's society, where youth equals beauty, a shiny pate is upsetting to a man who feels his good looks are receding with his hairline. Not surprisingly, hair replacement is a booming high-tech industry. Today men (and women) hang upside down, take drugs, splash medicine on their scalps, and receive laser-beam treatments in order to stimulate hair growth. Hair can be surgically transplanted and implanted. If that doesn't work, the oldest form of hair replacement, the wig, can still give the illusion of a full head of hair.

It is said that Julius Caesar always wore a wreath of gilded oak leaves to hide his baldness.

When the Roman poet Martial (A.D. 40–104) saw a friend had painted over his bald patch, he said: "You can cut your hair with a sponge!"

Today Americans can cover their bald patches in much the same way as the Romans: with a type of "spray paint."

In a transplant a plug or strip of hair is taken from the back of the head and implanted on the bald patch. But the result can look like doll's hair unless the surgeon is very skilled, and sometimes the procedure doesn't work, leaving the patient to live with the scars (right).

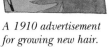

A 1910 advertisement for growing new hair.

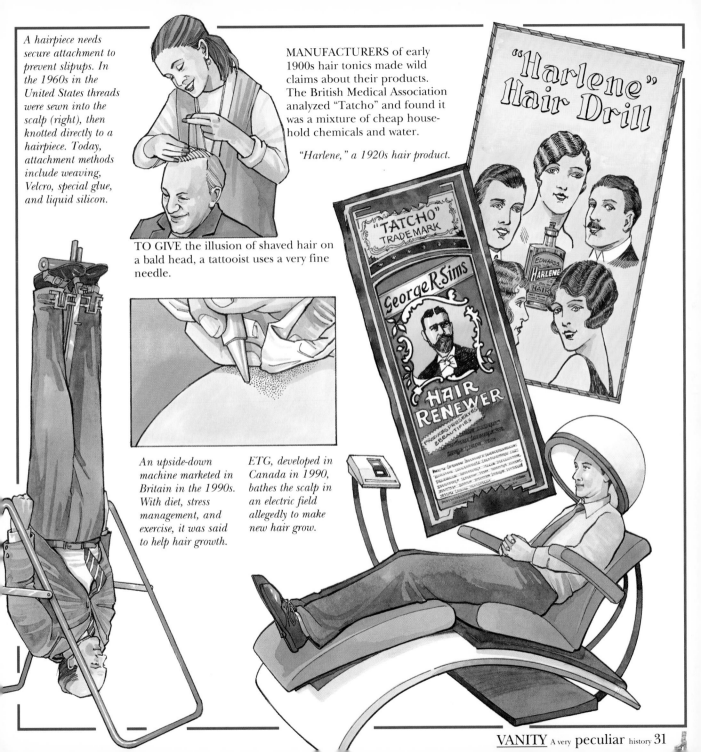

A hairpiece needs secure attachment to prevent slipups. In the 1960s in the United States threads were sewn into the scalp (right), then knotted directly to a hairpiece. Today, attachment methods include weaving, Velcro, special glue, and liquid silicon.

MANUFACTURERS of early 1900s hair tonics made wild claims about their products. The British Medical Association analyzed "Tatcho" and found it was a mixture of cheap household chemicals and water.

"Harlene," a 1920s hair product.

"Harlene" Hair Drill

"TATCHO" TRADE MARK

George R. Sims

HAIR RENEWER

PRODUCES PRESERVES BEAUTIFIES

TO GIVE the illusion of shaved hair on a bald head, a tattooist uses a very fine needle.

An upside-down machine marketed in Britain in the 1990s. With diet, stress management, and exercise, it was said to help hair growth.

ETG, developed in Canada in 1990, bathes the scalp in an electric field allegedly to make new hair grow.

BEARDS AND MUSTACHES

From virility to villainy, the beard makes the man.

Phoenician royals had their beards dyed, curled, scented, and even sprinkled with gold dust, c.1200 B.C.

RUSSIAN CZAR Peter the Great (1672–1725) banned beards (above), then relented and imposed a beard tax (left).

Johann Steiniger, a mayor in Austria, grew an 8.5-foot (2.6-m) beard. One day in 1567 he neglected to tuck it up, tripped over it, fell down the stairs, and died.

The Egyptian queen Hatshepsut wore a false beard as a sign of royalty, c.1480 B.C.

Alexander the Great's soldiers had to shave off their beards so the enemy could not catch hold of them, c.334 B.C.

T HE ISSUE OF BEARDS has occupied the minds of a good many men over the centuries, judging by the treatises devoted to the moral arguments for and against facial hair. The bearded man has been considered more godly, virile, and knowledgeable than other men, or, conversely, vainer and more pompous. Churches and kings have alternately railed against facial hair as filthy and vulgar, and embraced it as a sign of piety.

Among the ancient Egyptians, beards were reserved for men of rank, who sometimes shaved and wore false beards. Few Romans wore beards until Emperor Hadrian (ruled A.D. 117–138) grew one in A.D. 120 to cover his facial scars. Over the centuries, hundreds of different beard styles were adopted and abandoned, as were beards themselves, notably in the 18th and 20th centuries.

Beard styles became associated with certain professions. The pointed beard, or goatee, was popular with artists, untidy, flowing beards among poets, and rectangular beards among scientists.

In the 20th century, movie stars replaced rulers as the arbiters of fashion. Most are clean shaven, and beards have largely fallen out of fashion.

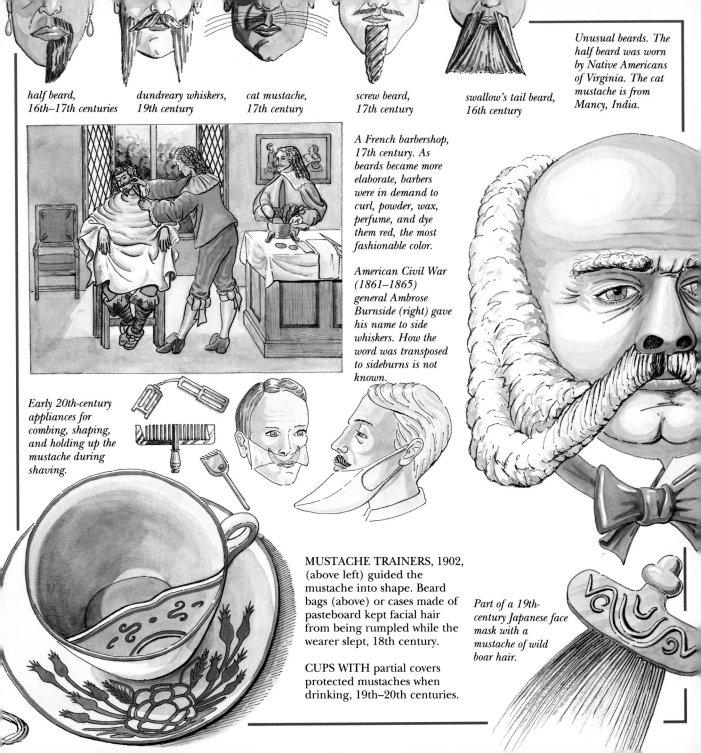

half beard,
16th–17th centuries

dundreary whiskers,
19th century

cat mustache,
17th century

screw beard,
17th century

swallow's tail beard,
16th century

Unusual beards. The half beard was worn by Native Americans of Virginia. The cat mustache is from Mancy, India.

A French barbershop, 17th century. As beards became more elaborate, barbers were in demand to curl, powder, wax, perfume, and dye them red, the most fashionable color.

American Civil War (1861–1865) general Ambrose Burnside (right) gave his name to side whiskers. How the word was transposed to sideburns is not known.

Early 20th-century appliances for combing, shaping, and holding up the mustache during shaving.

MUSTACHE TRAINERS, 1902, (above left) guided the mustache into shape. Beard bags (above) or cases made of pasteboard kept facial hair from being rumpled while the wearer slept, 18th century.

CUPS WITH partial covers protected mustaches when drinking, 19th–20th centuries.

Part of a 19th-century Japanese face mask with a mustache of wild boar hair.

VANITY WIGS

Who cares if it's hot and heavy, as long as it's fashionable?

Egyptian wigs were made from human hair or vegetable fiber and stiffened with beeswax.

In the 18th century, barbers ran through the streets of London and Paris to deliver wigs to wealthy customers.

Roman women had a penchant for blonde wigs. The hair came from conquered Germanic peoples.

Two monarchs started wearing wigs to disguise baldness. Elizabeth I had thinning hair (attributed by some to overuse of lead-based makeup), while Louis XIV began wearing a wig when he was 35 and balding. 18th-century Macaronis wore wigs with a queue, or tail, at the back.

Queen Elizabeth I

King Louis XIV

A Macaroni

powdered wig

powdered wig

THE ANCIENT EGYPTIANS shaved their heads and wore wigs for festive occasions and to denote rank and authority. Statues show that wig styles were subject to flights of fashion even five thousand years ago. By about 2000 B.C., the wigs were so huge that wearers became top-heavy, and needed help to walk.

Wigs were popular among ancient Roman women, since it was one of the few ways in which they could become blonde. But the Christian church's disapproval caused wigs to fall out of fashion. In the first century A.D., the Greek theologian Clement of Alexandria went so far as to say that a priest's blessing could not be received by a wig wearer, because the blessing would remain on top of the wig and not pass through to the wearer. In 692, Christian wig wearers were even excommunicated.

Queen Elizabeth I reintroduced the wig as a fashion item for women, but it was King Louis XIV of France (reigned 1643-1715) who catapulted wigs into undreamed-of fashion heights, where they remained for almost two centuries.

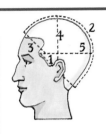

Measurements for a wig: 1. Circumference. 2. Forehead to nape. 3, 4. Ear to ear. 5. Temple to temple.

Tasks carried out in a wigmaker's workroom, 18th century:
1. Shaving a beard.
2. Making a wig.
3. Weaving hair onto strings of cotton.
4. Mounting a wig onto a wooden block.
5. Heating the crimping irons for curling the wig.
6. Man removing powder from his face.

Making a hairpiece worn at the front of the head. Hair was sometimes mounted on pig's or sheep's skin.

IN 17th-CENTURY London expensive wigs were snatched off heads by dogs or children hiding in baskets slung over the shoulder of an adult.

After a wig was greased, powder was applied using a puff or bellows. A cone or mask protected the face. The clothes were covered with a cloth, or else the wearer stepped into a powder room and stuck his or her head out of the curtains.

Hair powder has been made from flour, orris root (the rhizomes of a type of iris), nutmeg, starch, and gold dust. So much flour was used on the hair of French aristocrats that hungry peasants complained.

A tax on hair powder was introduced in England in 1795.

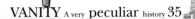

HAIR FASHIONS

A short history of hair-raising styles.

Roman style of 2nd century A.D. *A wire frame in front held the hair up.*

Bizarre hairstyle worn in Venice in the 15th century.

Big hairstyles were dangerous. A few women met their deaths after their coiffures collided with chandeliers and caught fire.

A large coiffure was expensive, so it had to last. Women preserved their hair by covering it and by sleeping sitting up.

Tall hairstyles required sedan chairs with roofs that opened. A retractable hairdo was even invented.

HAIR IS EASILY CUT, painlessly styled, and continually growing, making it the perfect fashion accessory. But wearing the latest style was not always easy. In ancient Egypt and Assyria, hairstyles were regulated by law. In ancient Rome a rich woman required a multitude of slaves to dress her hair. After the Middle Ages, the Renaissance heralded the re-emergence of complicated hairstyles. Nothing, however, could compare with the enormous coiffures, some as high as 30 inches (75 cm), worn by women in the 18th century. In 1776 the roof of the main entrance of St. Paul's Cathedral, London, was raised by 4 feet (1.2 m) to accommodate them. Even more amazing were the decorations: miniature tableaux of battles at sea or formal gardens with fresh flowers, all achieved by adding large amounts of false hair, padding, grease, flour, and powder to the hair.

Not surprisingly, the status of hairdressers grew, and from the 17th century their influence has meant that hair fashions have changed quickly. Where once a style had served a civilization for centuries, now a new coiffure was needed every few years.

ELABORATE HAIRSTYLES of the 18th and 19th centuries, including the chignon (below), required enormous quantities of false hair. It was supplied by peasants (right) who were paid a small fee.

THE HAIRSTYLES of Mangbetu women highlight their elongated skulls, achieved by wrapping the head from birth.

The beehive caught on in the United States around 1958. Hair was back-combed over a wire or plastic frame and held up with hairspray.

(right) Increasing emancipation in the early 20th century gave women greater freedom; though few were brave enough to adopt the style sketched here.

traditional African comb

Ancient Roman comb (below) with the name of its owner.

The emblem of punks is dyed, stiffened hair.

BEAR'S GREASE was a popular hair dressing for centuries, but it had a rancid smell and needed heavy perfuming.

WILLIAM CANNICOTT'S
Genuine
BEARS GREASE
for strengthening &
thickening the

Dreadlocks, an Ethiopian style of uncombed braided hair, are often worn by Rastafarians.

DRESSING HAIR

Early Greek men craved the "fragrant and divine curls" so often mentioned in their poetry, because complicated hairstyles set them apart from the short-haired northern barbarians.

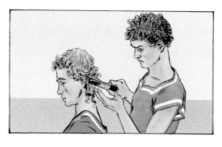

Hair can be dealt with as fashion dictates.

WHEN GREEK civilization reached its height around the 4th century B.C., hairstyles became increasingly elaborate. Hair was dressed with oil, perfume, and pomades, while a special mud was used to set curls. Dyes and powders colored hair gold, red, and white.

T O ACHIEVE the complicated hairstyles characteristic of most civilizations, extraordinary tools, methods, and preparations were used. The Assyrians elevated hairstyling to an art as early as 1500 B.C., crimping and oiling their hair. Changing hair color was another ancient preoccupation. It was perhaps the Greeks who invented the maxim "gentlemen prefer blondes," for Greeks lightened their locks by bleaching them with vinegar, sprinkling them with fine gold dust, or sitting in the sun. The Romans also craved the bleached-blond look. But early bleaches and dyes were notoriously unreliable, as shown by the words of Latin poet Ovid to his mistress: "Did I not say to thee, 'Cease to dye thy hair?' And now thou hast no longer any hair to dye." From the Romans to the Victorians and beyond, curls and ringlets, real and false, have been fashionable female adornments. Making curls last was a problem that was not solved until 1904, with the invention of the permanent waving machine. Since then, chemical compounds have been invented to straighten as well as curl hair, depending on the fashion.

A rich Roman woman had many slaves to dress her hair. Slaves called cinerarii *curled hair with heated tongs.* Cinflones *dyed hair by blowing powder through it.*

Not content with tattooing themselves blue with woad, Anglo-Saxon men and women also dyed their hair blue.

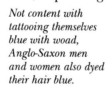

A 16th-century Venetian bleaches her hair by washing it in alkali and sitting in the sun to let it dry.

CRIMPED HAIR was a popular 19th-century style that could be achieved at home without crimping irons (below) by braiding a lock of hair and placing a hot iron on it.

crimping irons

Singeing the hair with a lighted taper, practiced in the 19th century, was said to seal the ends of the hair to prevent them bleeding.

IN 1872, French hairdresser Marcel Grateau (left) invented the permanent wave while experimenting on his mother's hair using heated curling irons. But the "marcel" wasn't permanent. Permanent waving machines (right), which became widely available in the 1920s, worked by heating chemically treated hair.

The beehive and bouffant styles of the 1950s and 1960s required so much preparation that women in rollers became a familiar sight in the street.

By the mid-1960s the beehive was out, and long, straight hair was in. Girls tried ironing it between two paper bags, but often scorched it.

HELPING HANDS

Egyptian queen Nefertiti sported red fingernails and toenails. The color of nail polish indicated social rank.

The manicured look.

In China during the Chou Dynasty, c.600 B.C., royals had long nails painted silver or gold, which they rested on cushions to prevent breakage.

Before battle, Babylonian officers c.1500 B.C. spent hours grooming their hair and beards and having their nails and lips painted.

Indian hand ornaments like this are believed to protect the wearer from bad luck.

I N EARLY CIVILIZATIONS well-cared-for hands distinguished the nobility from laboring peasants, whose hands were hardened by work. A manicure set was found in the royal tombs at Ur, which indicates that upper-class Babylonians were having manicures four thousand years ago. In ancient Egypt and India it was common for people to stain their fingernails and fingers red with henna.

The first nail polish, invented by the ancient Chinese, was a mixture of gum arabic, egg white, beeswax, and gelatin. In ancient China and Egypt the color of nail polish was associated with rank, with slaves usually forbidden to paint their nails at all. Brightly colored nails came into vogue again in Europe in the early 20th century.

But fingernails are not the only part of the hand to be decorated. In many tribal cultures the whole hand is painted because hands, along with the mouth and feet, are points of contact with the outside world, and so are considered sensitive areas. Middle Eastern and North African women often paint intricate patterns on their hands and feet with henna. Women of the Ainu tribe of Japan have their hands and mouth tattooed when they get married.

The Iban people of Borneo show prowess in war with tattoos, but only a warrior who takes a head can have his hands tattooed.

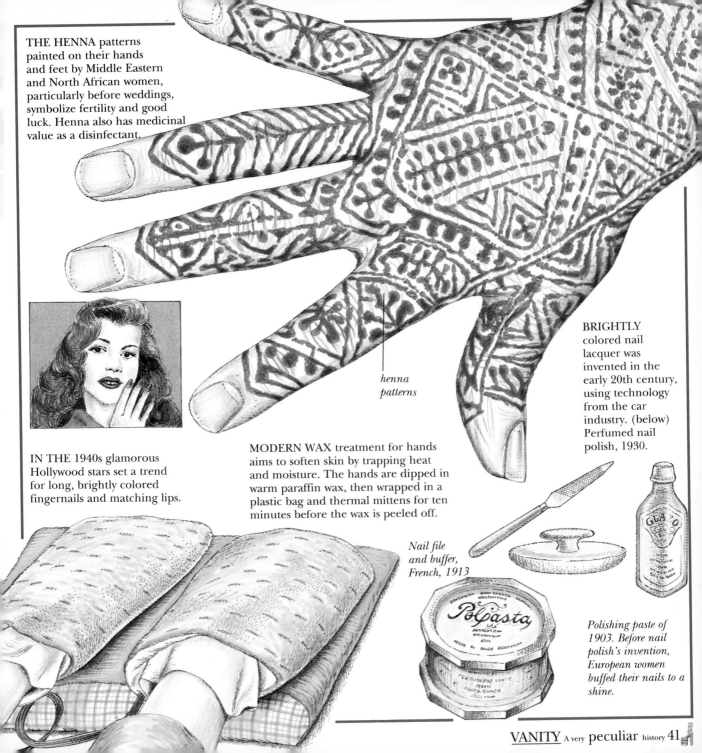

THE HENNA patterns painted on their hands and feet by Middle Eastern and North African women, particularly before weddings, symbolize fertility and good luck. Henna also has medicinal value as a disinfectant.

henna patterns

BRIGHTLY colored nail lacquer was invented in the early 20th century, using technology from the car industry. (below) Perfumed nail polish, 1930.

IN THE 1940s glamorous Hollywood stars set a trend for long, brightly colored fingernails and matching lips.

MODERN WAX treatment for hands aims to soften skin by trapping heat and moisture. The hands are dipped in warm paraffin wax, then wrapped in a plastic bag and thermal mittens for ten minutes before the wax is peeled off.

Nail file and buffer, French, 1913

Polpasta

Polishing paste of 1903. Before nail polish's invention, European women buffed their nails to a shine.

FOOTWORK

Putting fashion, not feet, first.

Ethiopian king's shoe allowing him to tread on his enemies, c.6th century B.C.

X-ray of foot

In the Middle Ages, a man's shoe, the poulaine, had a toe so long it was considered sexually suggestive.

X ray of bound foot

Long-toed shoes like this fishtail style were popular in England from the 11th to the 13th centuries.

Geta are traditional Japanese pedestal clogs. The highest geta were worn by emperors and courtesans.

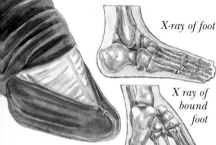

tiny shoes for bound feet

Foot-binding began in 10th-century China. Women with such distorted feet needed help to walk, a sign of social status. Foot-binding was banned in 1912.

Pattens, high heels of wood or metal, were introduced in the 16th century to help peasants negotiate muddy streets. Pattens never became very popular, as they were shunned by the élite.

SHOES WERE INVENTED to protect the feet, but even the earliest civilizations realized the fashion possibilities for footwear. The Egyptian queen Hatshepsut elevated the humble sandal to fashionable status by decorating hers with jewels. Roman women wore platform shoes during the time of Julius Caesar (102–44 B.C.), who himself wore high red boots trimmed with gold. Medieval Europeans designed some bizarre footwear, from the scandalously long-toed to the ridiculously wide. The small foot à la Cinderella has been fashionable for centuries. The Chinese took this to barbaric extremes by binding the feet of upper-class girls from the age of about four. It painfully forced the toes under the foot to make it only 5 inches (13 cm) long. Still, bound feet were considered aristocratic and desirable. In 19th-century Europe, many women had toes amputated to help them fit into fashionable, narrow shoes. During the Renaissance, rich European women were immobilized by wearing shoes built on stilts so high that they had to lean on their maids or be carried in sedan chairs. High heels were introduced in the 17th century and worn by both sexes, though men persevered for only a century.

Chopines (right) rose to fame in 16th-century Venice and were worn by the European élite for centuries despite efforts to ban them. With cork or leather soles 20 inches (50 cm) high, they made it impossible for women to walk unaided. (left) The skirt of a Venetian courtesan is cut away to reveal her shoes.

In Cinderella, small feet are considered aristocratic and feminine. Each of Cinderella's sisters tries to squash her big foot into the glass slipper (below).

Platforms originated in China and were worn by Roman women to make them taller. In the 1970s, glitter rock stars like Elton John catapulted them to new fashion heights.

In Syria these pedestal clogs, or kubkabs, are made extra high for brides as a way of showing their submission and helplessness.

Spike heels, or stilettos, are proof that comfort has not yet triumphed over fashion. Invented in Italy in the early 1950s and still worn today, shoes with these cigarette-thin heels make the bottom stick out and cause a zigzag posture. Their appeal is in the unnatural, sexy walk they force the wearer to adopt.

MIRROR, MIRROR...

Beau Brummell (1778–1840) The original English dandy, Brummell possessed exquisite dress sense, which influenced men's fashion in Europe for a hundred years. A friend of the Prince Regent (later George IV), Brummell shaved or plucked his face several times a day, bathed regularly (a novelty at the time), shunned all makeup, and employed three hairdressers. He cultivated an affected and snobbish manner that eventually offended the king, causing him to fall out of favor and die penniless and mad.

Sarah Bernhardt (1844–1923) She used makeup lavishly, whitening her face with powder, darkening her eyes, and scandalizing Victorian society by applying lip rouge in public.

Catherine de Médici (1519–1589) Wife of King Henry II of France, she is said to be the inventor of the iron corset and the rigid "corps," a wooden corset that went right up to the neck. Legend has it that she prescribed a 13-inch (33-cm) waist for all court members.

Benjamin Disraeli (1804–1881) Best known as a statesman and author, as a young man Disraeli defied Brummell-inspired fashion to dress ostentatiously, appearing at one party in purple trousers with a gold stripe, a scarlet waistcoat, gold chains, rings over his gloves, and his hair in long black ringlets.

George IV (1762–1830) Prince Regent from 1820 to 1830. Legend has it that he burst into tears when his friend Beau Brummell told him that his breeches did not fit. He wore a corset, chalked his cheeks and even applied leeches to tone down his ruddy complexion.

Maria Gunning A London society beauty in the 1750s, Maria could not be dissuaded from using white lead makeup and died at the age of 27.

Hadrian (76–138) Roman emperor who wore a wig to cover his baldness and revived the beard to hide his facial scars.

King Henry III of France (1551–1589) He used cosmetics on his face, eyes, and ears, wore a wig to hide a hair-dyeing disaster, and sported front teeth made of bone.

Hippocrates (460–c.377 B.C.) Greek physician who tried to reverse baldness by bathing his scalp in a mixture of opium, pigeon excrement, spices, and perfumes.

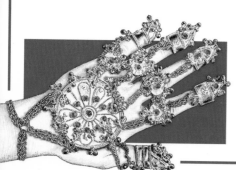

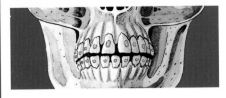

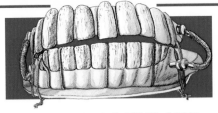

Isabella The wife of French king Charles VI (reigned 1380–1422) is said to have shed fat by sweating it out in special hot rooms.

Jezebel The queen of Hebrew king Ahab (reigned c.874–c.853 B.C.) was criticized for wearing heavy makeup, which contributed to her reputation as the archetypal wicked woman.

Julius Caesar (100–44 B.C.) He was never seen in public without a wreath of gilded oak leaves on his head to hide his baldness and was criticized for trying to look young by wearing high red boots trimmed with gold.

Louis XIV (1638–1715) The French king added high heels to his shoes because he was short, but his fawning courtiers emulated him, forcing Louis to wear ever higher heels.

Mary ("Queen of Scots") Stuart (1542–87) Vain to the bitter end, she went to her execution in "borrowed" hair. The wig fell off as her head fell from the block.

Narcissus In Greek mythology, a beautiful boy who spurned love. As punishment, a curse was put upon him to fall in love with his own reflection and pine away until he turned into a flower.

Peter the Great (1672–1725) So image-conscious was Peter that in 1698, after returning from a tour of Europe, he personally cut off the beards of his nobles and forced them to wear European clothes like his own.

Poppaea Wife of Roman emperor Nero (reigned 54–68). She polished her teeth with pumice stone, covered her face with white lead, painted her cheeks and lips with a red poison called fucus, lined her eyes with antimony, and drew blue veins on her bosom. She went to bed in a face pack made of meal, and in the morning bathed in asses' milk. She bleached her freckles with lemon juice and her hair with hessian soap. Yet despite these efforts to make herself beautiful, Nero killed her.

Queen Elizabeth I (1533–1603) Among the monarch's fashion foibles were painting her face and breasts with white lead and drawing blue veins on them to simulate the translucent skin of a much younger woman. She plucked her eyebrows and forehead according to fashion, and later wore a curly red wig to disguise thinning hair. She carried wads of cotton in her mouth to puff up her cheeks sunken by rotting teeth. She was particularly proud of her hands, which were long and delicate. She always made sure they featured in the many portraits painted of her.

George Washington (1732–99) Plagued by troubles with his teeth, the first American president wore artificial teeth, which altered the expression on his face when having his portrait painted.

GLOSSARY

bustle A fake posterior worn by women, made of a stuffed pad or a wire or whalebone basket. It was tied around the waist to simulate a large bottom and was fashionable in Europe and the United States from 1870 to 1890.

calf pads Used by men to create a more shapely leg in the early 19th century, when coats became shorter.

ceruse Lethal makeup to whiten the face made from lead, vinegar, and egg white; used for centuries in ancient civilizations and in Europe until the 18th century. The best ceruse, which also contained the highest proportion of lead, came from Venice. It ate into the skin, requiring ever thicker applications, while the lead was steadily absorbed into the blood, often causing death.

chest wig A lightweight wig used to disguise a hairless chest on the beach, advertised in the United States in the 1920s.

chignon A large coil of hair usually worn at the nape of the neck.

codpiece A bag or flap that concealed the gap at the top of men's hose when coats became shorter in the 15th and 16th centuries. Codpieces were stiffened, decorated, and, according to legend, used to hide jewels and bonbons.

crimping Frizzing or waving the hair using a curling iron.

dandy A term applied to men of the 19th century who dressed flamboyantly, often used makeup, and behaved in an affected, snobbish manner. The true dandy as personified by Beau Brummell (see page 44), however, wore no makeup and dressed in an immaculate way intended to be inconspicuous.

electrolysis A technique, pioneered in the 1940s, of removing unwanted hair by destroying the hair roots. A fine needle is applied to the roots and a small electric current is passed through. It is painful, but with a good practitioner the results are usually permanent.

ETG (Electro Tricho Genesis) A way of growing hair by applying low-impulse electrostatic current to the scalp. It was developed after a California electro-acupuncturist discovered that, as a side effect of treatment, his patients were growing new hair. ETG patients bathe their scalp for twelve minutes once a week for up to two years. Nobody knows exactly how the treatment works.

eyebrows Have risen and fallen with fashion and sometimes disappeared altogether. The ancient Egyptians shaved them, then drew them on with kohl. In ancient Rome and Persia the most attractive eyebrows met in the middle. In the 15th and 16th centuries, women plucked their eyebrows and hairlines. In the 1930s severely plucked eyebrows were made popular by Greta Garbo and Marlene Dietrich.

hair removal (see also **electrolysis**) Ancient methods, some of which are still used today, include plucking, rubbing with pumice stone, singeing, sugaring (ripping hair out after applying a thick honeylike substance), waxing, and applying depilatories. Some ancient depilatories were made from substances such as cat's dung and crushed eggshells. Ancient Greeks and Romans used orpiment, a dangerous depilatory made from arsenic.

henna The powdered leaves of a plant that, when mixed with water, has been used for centuries to dye the hair or body red or auburn.

Macaronis A group of young Englishmen who, after spending time in Italy, took on the name in the 1760s and 1770s as a rebellion against their elders. Macaronis wore exaggerated versions of fashionable clothes, elaborate makeup, and large powdered wigs with a tiny tricorn hat on top.

Maya A sophisticated ancient civilization of Mexico, Belize, and northern Guatemala that probably originated c.1000 B.C. but was dying out when conquered by the Spanish in 1546.

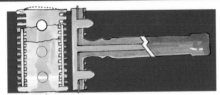

mirrors Egyptian mirrors of c.2800 B.C. were made of polished bronze, silver, or gold. The use of glass mirrors was first recorded in Europe in the 7th century, and they were widely used by the 14th century.

moko Form of tattooing used by the Maoris of New Zealand. Instead of a needle, a chisel and light mallet were used to incise the complex curls and spirals that characterize the designs. Black pigment was then rubbed into the cuts. Maoris believed that their personalities were imprinted on their moko facial designs, and Maori chiefs drew their face designs as their signature.

patches Pieces of silk, taffeta, or leather in the shape of crescent moons, stars, even a coach and horses, worn on the face. Popular with the ancient Romans and 17th-century European aristocrats, patches, mostly in black or scarlet, hid smallpox scars and were also purely decorative. Among members of King Louis XIV's court in France, a patch on the left cheek indicated that a woman was engaged; on the right cheek that she was married. A patch near the lip was flirtatious.

peasecod belly A false paunch, thought to improve a man's figure, attained by stuffing the shirt. It was worn by European men in the 16th century.

toothpaste Ancient Egyptian toothpaste was made from powdered pumice stone and vinegar, while Romans cleaned their teeth with urine. 18th-century teeth whiteners included gunpowder, salt, and soot. Fluoride was first used in Italy in the 1840s and added to drinking water in the United States in 1915.

woad Blue dye from the dried leaves of plants from the Isatis genus.

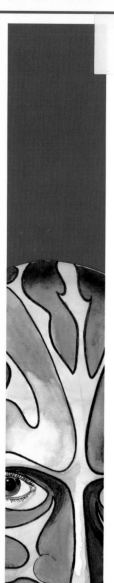

Artists

David Antram, pages 14–15, 20–21, 28–29, 30–31, 34–35, 38–39; Ray Burrows, pages 40–41; Virginia Gray, pages 12–13; Nick Hewetson, pages 36–37; Barbara Loftus, pages 8–9, 10–11; Gordon Munro, pages 16–17; Lee Peters, pages 18–19, 24–25, 26–27, 32–33; Carolyn Scrace, pages 22–23, 42–43.